Vehicles
On The Move

FIGHTER JETS
Defending the Skies

Lynn Peppas

🍄 Crabtree Publishing Company

www.crabtreebooks.com

Created by Bobbie Kalman

Dedicated By Samara Parent
for my newest nephew Nathan, be the pilot of your dreams. xoxo

Author
Lynn Peppas

Editor
Adrianna Morganelli

Proofreader
Kathy Middleton

Photo research
Samara Parent

Design
Samara Parent

**Production coordinator
and prepress technician**
Samara Parent

Print coordinator
Katherine Berti

Photographs
iStockphoto.com: © Chris Parypa (page 12 bottom)
Shutterstock.com: © Derek Gordon (title page, table of contents);
   ©Piotr Zajc (pages 4-5, top 8-13 top, 15-16 top, 20-21 top, 24-25 top, 27-31 top);
   © Sascha Hahn (pages 6-7); © dcwcreations (pages 8, 9); © Ajay Bhaskar
   (page 11 middle); © ernstc (page 11 bottom); © Dan Simonsen
   (pages 12 middle, 15); © B747 (page 13); © Karl R. Martin (page 14);
   © John Steel (page 20 middle); © Brynteg (page 26); © Graham Taylor
   (page 27 middle); © Craig Wactor (page 28);
Lockheed Martin: David Drais (page 4)
U.S. Air Force: Staff Sgt. Brian Ferguson (page 5)
Wikimedia commons: © Paul Maritz (page 10 middle); page 24; U.S.
   Government: front cover, back cover, pages 10 bottom, 16, 17, 18-19, 20,
   21, 22-23 both, 25 both, 27, 29, 30-31 both

Front cover: An F-35 Joint Strike Fighter lands at Edwards Air Force Base in California.
Back cover: An F-117 Nighthawk
Title page: A flight crew member directs a F-18 Hornet fighter jet onto an aircraft carrier.

Library and Archives Canada Cataloguing in Publication

Peppas, Lynn
   Fighter jets : defending the skies / Lynn Peppas.

(Vehicles on the move)
Includes index.
Issued also in electronic formats.
ISBN 978-0-7787-2748-4 (bound).--ISBN 978-0-7787-2753-8 (pbk.)

   1. Jet fighter planes--Juvenile literature.
I. Title. II. Series: Vehicles on the move

UG1242.F5P46 2011   j623.74'64   C2011-906714-5

Library of Congress Cataloging-in-Publication Data

Peppas, Lynn.
   Fighter jets : defending the skies / Lynn Peppas.
      p. cm. -- (Vehicles on the move)
   Includes index.
   ISBN 978-0-7787-2748-4 (reinforced library binding : alk. paper) --
ISBN 978-0-7787-2753-8 (pbk. : alk. paper) -- ISBN 978-1-4271-9926-3
(electronic pdf) -- ISBN 978-1-4271-9931-7 (electronic html)
   1. Jet fighter planes--Juvenile literature. I. Title. II. Series.

UG1242.F5P466 2012
623.74'64--dc23

2011039690

Crabtree Publishing Company

www.crabtreebooks.com   1-800-387-7650

Printed in the U.S.A./112011/JA20111018

Published in Canada
Crabtree Publishing
616 Welland Ave.
St. Catharines, Ontario
L2M 5V6

Published in the United States
Crabtree Publishing
PMB 59051
350 Fifth Avenue, 59th Floor
New York, New York 10118

Published in the United Kingdom
Crabtree Publishing
Maritime House
Basin Road North, Hove
BN41 1WR

Published in Australia
Crabtree Publishing
3 Charles Street
Coburg North
VIC 3058

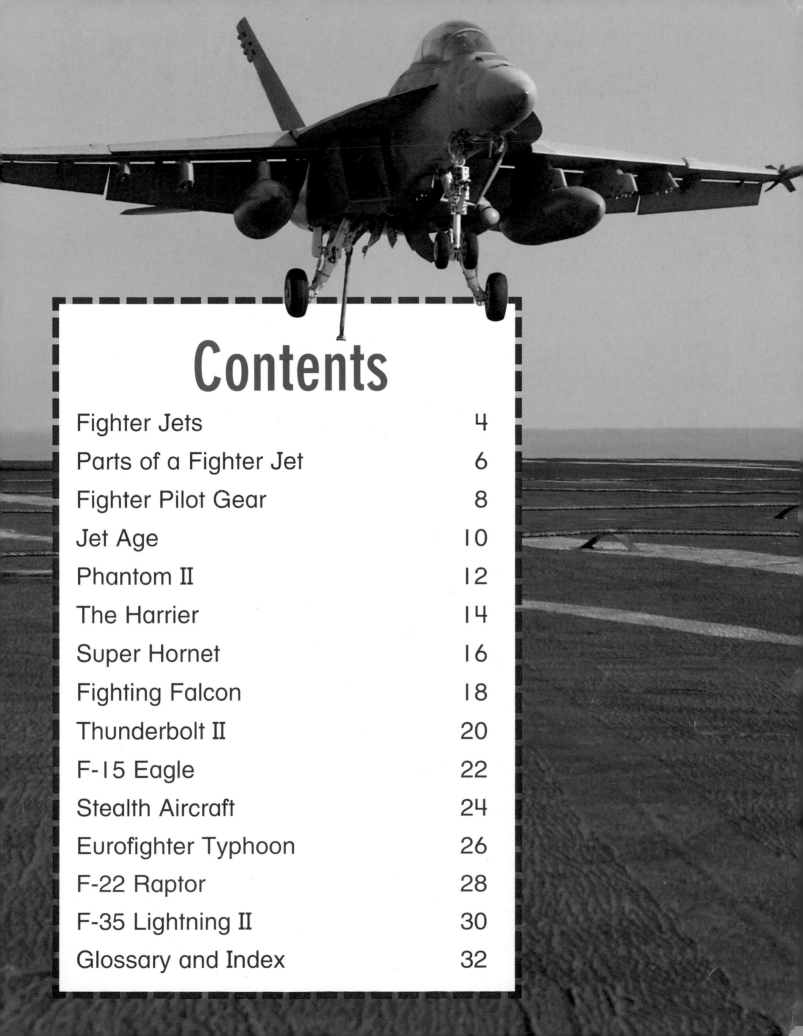

Contents

Fighter Jets

Fighter jets are **military** vehicles that fly. A military vehicle is a machine used by a country's **armed forces** to move people or do jobs. Sometimes fighter jets are called fighter aircraft or attack aircraft. Only specially trained pilots in the armed forces can fly a fighter jet.

New fighter jets are designed using the newest technologies in flying and weapons. This F-35 Lightning II is still being tested. It will be used by the military in 2016.

Fighter jets fly over an area to **spy**, or find things out. They also attack **enemy** aircraft in the air. Some jets attack enemy forces on the ground. Some drop bombs or **missiles**. Fighter jets are small and extremely fast. They can **maneuver**, or change the direction they are flying, easily.

Fighter jets, like these F-22 Raptors, are some of the most expensive vehicles in the world.

Parts of a Fighter Jet

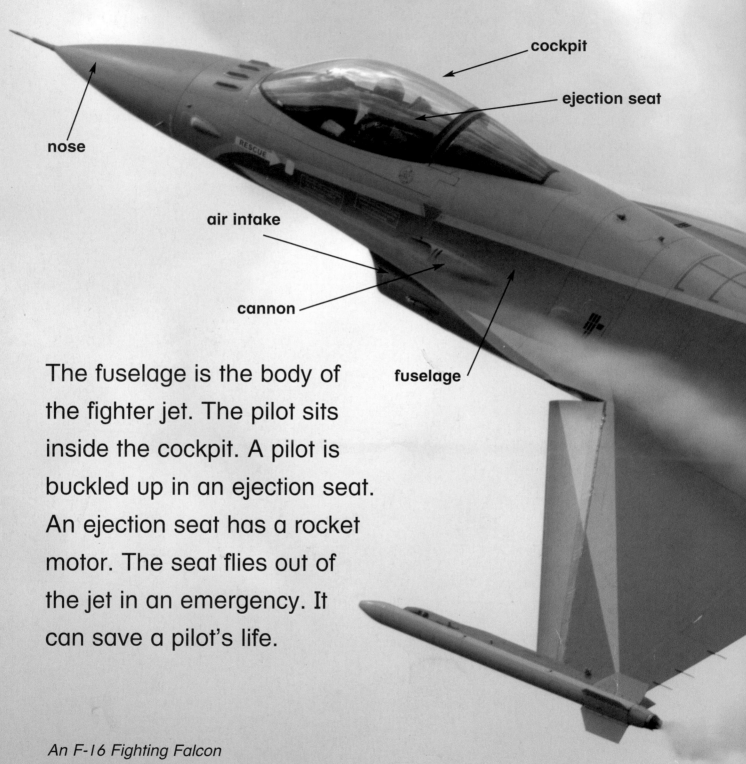

cockpit

ejection seat

nose

air intake

cannon

fuselage

The fuselage is the body of the fighter jet. The pilot sits inside the cockpit. A pilot is buckled up in an ejection seat. An ejection seat has a rocket motor. The seat flies out of the jet in an emergency. It can save a pilot's life.

An F-16 Fighting Falcon

Some fighter jets have swept-back wings that help them fly faster. Weapons such as bombs and missiles are kept underneath the jet in the wings or fuselage. A gun or **cannon** is kept in the nose or wings of a fighter jet.

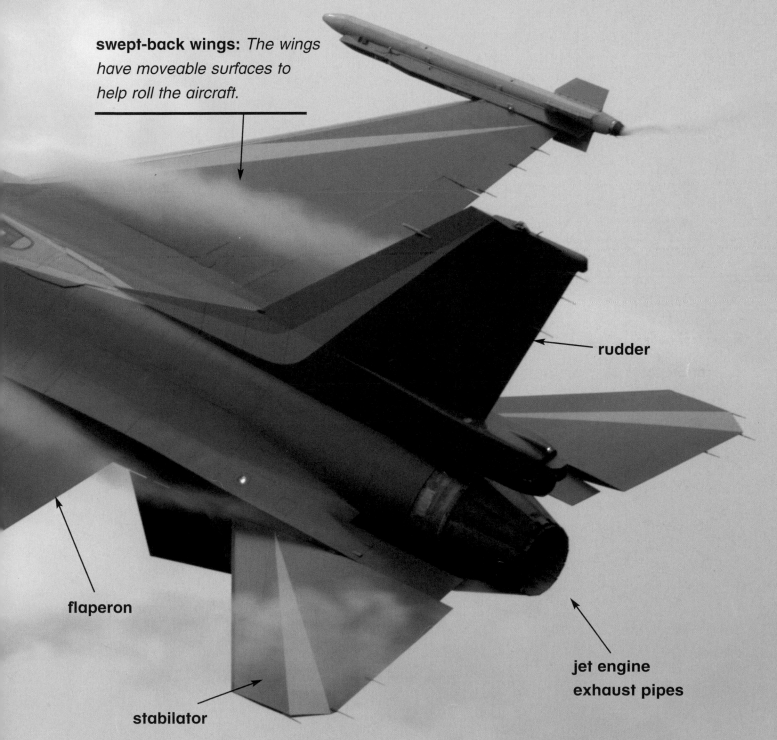

swept-back wings: *The wings have moveable surfaces to help roll the aircraft.*

rudder

flaperon

stabilator

jet engine exhaust pipes

Fighter Pilot Gear

Flying a fighter jet is a hard job. Pilots need to wear special gear to keep them safe. They wear a special helmet and an **oxygen** mask to help the pilot breathe when the jet flies far up in the sky.

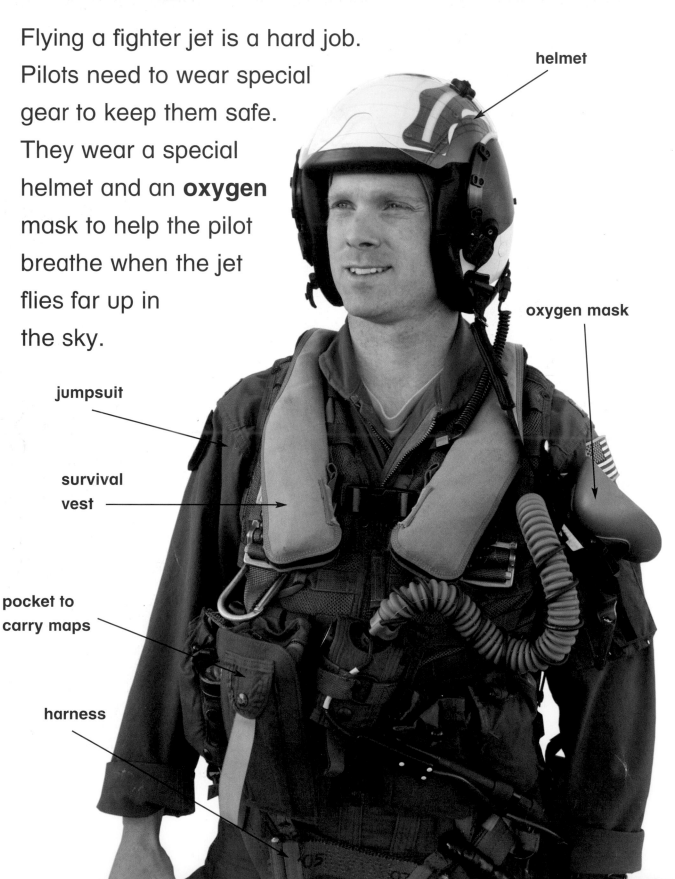

helmet

oxygen mask

jumpsuit

survival vest

pocket to carry maps

harness

When a fighter jet turns, dives, or climbs quickly, the jet and the pilot feel a lot of extra weight. This is called G-force. The letter G stands for **gravity**, and the force is the change in speed the pilot feels. This extra pressure can make a pilot **black out**. Pilots wear G-pants to fight the effects of G-force.

Fighter pilots train for many years. They must get top marks in school, and be healthy and physically fit.

Jet Age

The first fighter jet flew in 1942. Jet-powered engines made fighter aircraft travel a lot faster. In 1947, the F-86 Sabrejet was one of the first fighter jets made in the United States. At the time, it held the world speed record when it traveled 570 mph (920 km/h).

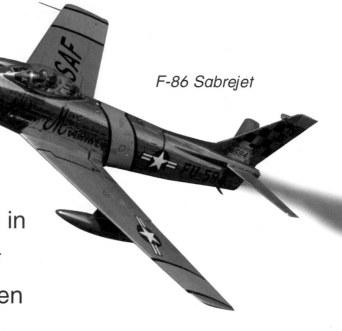

F-86 Sabrejet

F-86 Sabrejets were used during the Korean War from 1950 to 1953.

Fighter jet engines need **jet fuel** and air to make them move. The aircraft sucks air into the engine through an opening called the air intake. The air is sprayed with fuel and burned. The burning fuel blasts through a **nozzle** at the back of the engine. It pushes the aircraft forward at very fast speeds.

jet engine

An F-16 Fighting Falcon

air intake

Phantom II

The F-4 Phantom II is a supersonic jet. Supersonic means it can travel faster than the speed of sound. Sound travels at about 768 mph (1,236 km/h). The F-4 Phantom II can travel at speeds of up to 1,472 mph (2,370 km/h).

The nose on these two Phantoms have been painted with fierce faces.

The F-4 Phantom II first flew in 1958. At the time, it set world records for speed. It carries **air-to-air** and **air-to-ground** missiles. It has a cannon that fires over 6,000 rounds, or shots, in a minute.

The F-4 Phantom II cost more than two million dollars to make back in the 1960s.

cannon

The Harrier

The Harrier does not need a long **runway** to take off from or land on. It can take off or land straight up or down, like a helicopter. It does this with four jet-powered nozzles on the sides of its body. When the nozzles are turned downward the jet **hovers**. When it is up in the air the pilot turns the nozzles backward to move the jet forward fast.

This AV-8B Harrier II is hovering over a runway.

Special Functions

The Harrier can take off or land from an **aircraft carrier**. Sometimes it is called a Harrier Jump Jet. It carries a lot of weapons underneath its wings. It carries sidewinder missiles, bombs, and cannons.

The Sea Harrier FA2 (above) was used by the British Royal Navy until 2006. Harrier jets are no longer being produced, but some, such as the AV-8B, are still being used.

Super Hornet

The Super Hornet is a multi-role fighter jet. Multi-role means it can do many different jobs. It can get fuel from another aircraft while flying in the air. It can also give fuel to other aircraft, too. The Super Hornet attacks other aircraft in the air or helps forces on the ground. It carries many different weapons such as missiles, bombs, and a cannon.

A Super Hornet refuels.

High-speed Hornets

The Super Hornet is fast. It can change direction and make turns quickly, too. It can fly up to speeds of 1,190 mph (1,915 km/h). The price of one Super Hornet is 55 million dollars.

Fighting Falcon

The F-16 Fighting Falcon is
a dogfighter. That means it
fights enemy aircraft in the
air. The Falcon can
make difficult
moves at top
speeds. It can travel up to
1,500 mph (2,415 km/h), or
twice the speed of sound.

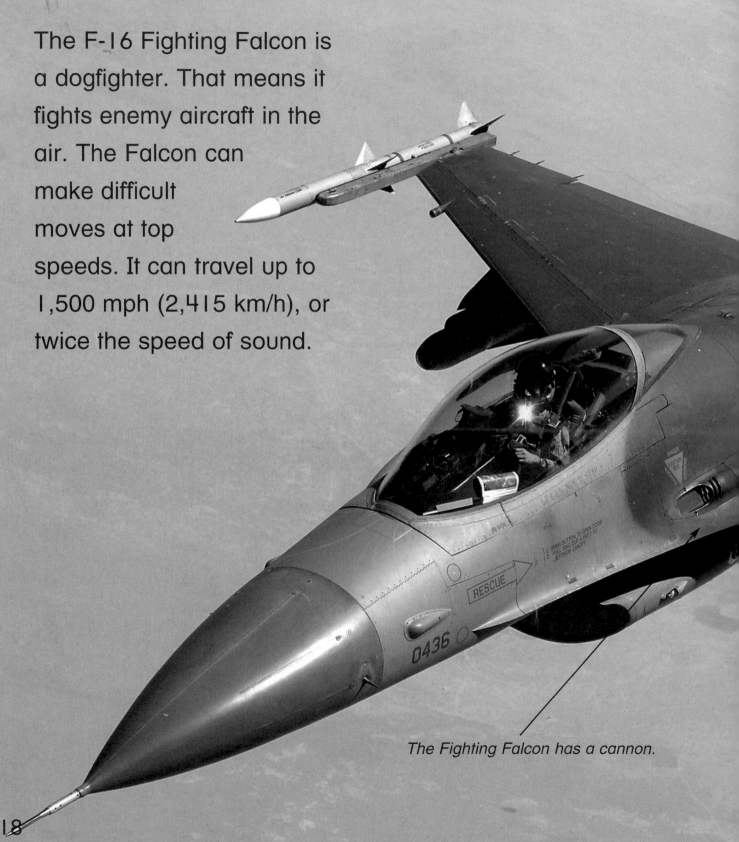

The Fighting Falcon has a cannon.

Piloting the Falcon

The Falcon is made for one pilot. The dome over the cockpit is shaped like a bubble. It helps the pilot see all around. One Fighting Falcon costs about 30 million dollars. It is not as expensive as some other fighter jets.

Thunderbolt II

The A-10 Thunderbolt II's nickname is the Warthog. A warthog is a wild pig with four tusks, or horns, coming from its mouth. Both the fighter jet and the animal are tough.

The A-10 has a 19-foot cannon sticking out of the nose.

The Fighting Warthog

The Warthog fights enemy forces on the ground. It attacks tanks and other **armored** vehicles. The pilot is protected by a special armor built into the aircraft. It also has a Night Vision Imaging System, which is equipment that helps the pilot fly in the dark.

The Warthog can travel up to 420 mph (675 km/h). It cannot break the speed of sound.

F-15 Eagle

The F-15 Eagle first flew in 1972. Since then, it has become the most successful fighter in the sky. It can move quickly and easily. It can fly up to 1,875 mph (3,018 km/h). It carries air-to-air weapons such as missiles and a gun that fires 940 rounds in one minute. The Eagle costs over 52 million dollars.

F-15 Eagle

A New Eagle

A new F-15 Strike Eagle was made in 1989. It is different from the regular F-15 Eagle because it is made to fight ground forces, too. It carries missiles, bombs, and a cannon. It can fly as fast as a regular F-15 Eagle.

Stealth Aircraft

Stealth aircraft are able to sneak by enemy **radar** without being seen. Stealth fighters look very different. They are covered in flat panels placed at different angles. This shape helps them block enemy radar systems. They are also covered with a special material called RAM. This material sucks in radar waves but does not let them bounce back off the plane.

F-117 Nighthawks

The Nighthawk

The F-117 Nighthawk is a stealth fighter. It carries one pilot. It holds bombs inside the aircraft. It can travel up to speeds of 617 mph (993 km/h). Designed for attacking targets on the ground, it does not fight other aircraft in the air.

This Nighthawk drops a laser-guided bomb on its target during a test. No longer being produced, the Nighthawk is being replaced by the F-22 Raptor and F-35 Lightning II.

Eurofighter Typhoon

The Eurofighter Typhoon can do many different jobs in the military. The name "Euro" comes from the European countries, such as the United Kingdom, Germany, Spain, and Italy, that helped to make them. The Typhoon is flown by one pilot and can travel up to 1,550 mph (2,495 km/h).

canard

The Eurofighter has small wings, called canards, at the front of the aircraft. Canards help the jet stabilize, or hold itself steady.

The Fighting Typhoon

One Typhoon costs about 128 million dollars. It has a cannon that can fire 1,700 rounds a minute. It is used for ground or air attacks, and carries missiles and bombs.

(above) The Eurofighter does not store weapons inside the aircraft. Bombs and missiles are attached underneath the wings.

F-22 Raptor

The F-22 Raptor first flew in 1990. A raptor is a bird that preys on, or hunts, other animals. The Raptor is one of the newest and most advanced fighter jets today. It is super-maneuverable and very fast. It is a stealth aircraft, too.

The Rapid Raptor

The Raptor seats only one. It can get up to speeds of 1,500 mph (2,415 km/h). It is used to attack enemy forces on the ground or in the air. The Raptor has a cannon that can fire 6,000 rounds every minute. Missiles and bombs are carried inside the jet in an area called a weapons bay.

The Raptor is built in the United States. A Raptor costs about 150 million dollars.

F-35 Lightning II

The Lightning II Joint Strike Fighter first flew in 2006. It is still being tested and worked on by the U.S. Department of Defense. The United States plans to use them in the military by the year 2016.

One model of the F-35 Lightning does regular takeoffs and landings. A second model can take off from aircraft carriers at sea. A third model can hover like the Harrier.

As Fast as Lightning

The Lightning II seats one pilot and travels at speeds up to 1,200 mph (1,930 km/h). It has a cannon that can shoot 4,000 rounds every minute. It carries a lot of missiles and bombs. It is a stealth aircraft, too.

cockpit

Glossary

aircraft carrier A military vehicle that carries aircraft and acts as a runway for them to take off or land

air-to-air/air-to-ground Type of weapon launched from the air toward a target in the air or on the ground

armed forces A country's group of soldiers who fight on the ground, at sea, and in the air

armor A protective material that acts as a shield

black out To lose consciousness

cannon A large, metal tube that fires explosive shells

enemy A force that works against a person or a country

gravity Earth's natural pull on objects

hover To hang still in the air

jet fuel A special mixture of products that gives jets power

maneuver To be able to change position, direction, or speed quickly

military A country's armed forces

missile An explosive weapon that is shot at a target in the distance

nozzle An exhaust duct, or tube, at the back of an engine

oxygen An element in the air that plants and animals need to live

radar A way of locating objects by bouncing radio waves off of them

runway A strip of level ground from which aircraft take off and land

spy To gather information secretly by observing

Index

10